Dash Diet Meal Prep for Beginners

<u>1000-Day Make-Ahead, Low-Salt Dash Diet Recipes to Promote Weight Loss Naturally and Lower Your Blood Pressure Together （A Cookbook）</u>

Segaon Cukey

© Copyright 2021 Segaon Cukey - All Rights Reserved.

In no way is it legal to reproduce, duplicate, or transmit any part of this document by either electronic means or in printed format. Recording of this publication is strictly prohibited, and any storage of this material is not allowed unless with written permission from the publisher. All rights reserved.

The information provided herein is stated to be truthful and consistent, in that any liability, regarding inattention or otherwise, by any usage or abuse of any policies, processes, or directions contained within is the solitary and complete responsibility of the recipient reader. Under no circumstances will any legal liability or blame be held against the publisher for any reparation, damages, or monetary loss due to the information herein, either directly or indirectly.

Respective authors own all copyrights not held by the publisher.

Legal Notice:

This book is copyright protected. This is only for personal use. You cannot amend, distribute, sell, use, quote or paraphrase any part of the content within this book without the consent of the author or copyright owner. Legal action will be pursued if this is breached.

Disclaimer Notice:

Please note the information contained within this document is for educational and entertainment purposes only. Every attempt has been made to provide accurate, up-to-date and reliable, complete information. No warranties of any kind are expressed or implied. Readers acknowledge that the author is not engaging in the rendering of legal, financial, medical or professional advice.

By reading this document, the reader agrees that under no circumstances are we responsible for any losses, direct or indirect, which are incurred as a result of the use of information contained within this document, including, but not limited to, errors, omissions, or inaccuracies.

Table of Contents

Introduction 7
Chapter 1: Overview of Dash Diet... **8**
    What is the Dash Diet? 8
    Benefits of Dash Diet 8
    Foods to Eat 9
    Tips for Getting Started 9
Chapter 2: 30-Day Meal Plan **12**
Chapter 3: Breakfast Recipes **18**
    Cheesy Frittata 18
    Breakfast Biscuits 19
    Flaxseed French Toast with Strawberries 20
    Hash Browns 21
    Breakfast Sausage 22
    Egg Tarts 23
    Breakfast Casserole 24
    Breakfast Peppers 25
    Breakfast Stuffed Pastries 26
    Broccoli & Cheese Quiche 27
Chapter 4: Chicken Recipes **28**
    Crispy Chicken Breast 28
    Chicken & Broccoli 30
    Mexican Chicken Wings 31
    Crunchy Chicken Tenderloins 32
    General Tso's Chicken 33
    Roast Chicken 35
    Korean Fried Chicken 36
    Buttermilk Fried Chicken 38
    Parmesan Chicken 40

  Lemon Chicken 41

Chapter 5: Meat Recipes **42**

  Rib Eye Steak 42

  Mustard Pork Tenderloin 43

  Ranch Pork Chops 44

  Lamb Chops with Mustard & Garlic 45

  Garlic & Rosemary Lamb Chops 46

  Meatballs 47

  Sausages 48

  Juicy Steaks 49

  Roast Beef 50

  Pork Chops & Brussels Sprouts 51

Chapter 6: Fish & Seafood Recipes **52**

  Sesame Cod & Snap Peas 52

  Coconut Shrimp 54

  Fish Cakes 56

  Lemon Paprika Shrimp 57

  Crispy Fish 58

  Salmon with Horseradish Rub 59

  Garlic Popcorn Shrimp 60

  Calamari 62

  Scallops with Lemon Herb Sauce 63

  Salmon Cakes with Spicy Mayo 64

Chapter 7: Vegetarian Recipes **65**

  Brussels Sprouts with Bacon 65

  Baked Potatoes with Broccoli 66

  Roasted Vegetables 67

  Baked Potatoes 68

  Falafel 69

  Eggplant Parmesan 70

Spicy Green Beans 72

Roasted Okra 73

Onion Rings 74

Crispy Green Tomatoes 76

Chapter 8: Snack Recipes 78

Curried Chickpeas 78

Pickle Chips 79

Sesame Kale Chips 80

Potato Chips 81

Roasted Peanuts 82

Fish & Chips 83

Greek Feta Fries 85

Cinnamon Plantain Chips 87

Zucchini Chips 88

Spicy Potato Wedges 90

Chapter 9: Appetizer Recipes 91

Scallops with Bacon 91

Stuffed Peppers 93

Tofu Bites 94

Pork Dumplings 95

Buffalo Wings 97

Egg Rolls 99

Jalapeño Poppers 100

Sausage Bites 101

Peppers Stuffed with Sausage 102

Mac & Cheese Balls 103

Chapter 10: Side Dish Recipes 104

Roasted Cauliflower & Broccoli 104

Cauliflower Gnocchi 105

Garlic Baby Potatoes 106

    Orange & Sesame Tofu 107
    Roasted Butternut Squash 108
Conclusion... 109

Introduction

With down-to-earth advice and a collection of delectable recipes to try, this practical guide breaks down the Dash diet in a way that anyone can understand, arming you with the essential tools and knowledge you need to transform your wellbeing and begin feeling the benefits of a healthier lifestyle.

Combining a proven 30-day meal plan with a selection of healthy, easy-to-prepare recipes for breakfast, lunch, dinner, dessert, snacks and more, the Dash diet helps you feel stronger and live better in a natural and intuitive way.

This Dash Diet Meal Prep for Beginners allows you to easily find foods you can eat more balanced and nutritious, and you can have the tasty meals at home without much effort.

Chapter 1: Overview of Dash Diet

What is the Dash Diet?

Dietary Approaches to Stop Hypertension (DASH) is a type of eating plan that is specifically designed to help people prevent high blood pressure without the use of any medication.

High blood pressure or hypertension affects at least 1 billion people in the world, with low to middle-income countries having the greatest prevalence. In the United States, 45 percent of adults suffer from high blood pressure and rely heavily on medication.

High blood pressure can cause serious problems if left uncontrolled. It can overwork your heart and cause permanent damage causing a series of problems to other vital organs. Elevated blood pressures can increase your risk of heart, kidney, brain, and eye diseases, among others.

The Dash diet mainly focuses on minimizing the consumption of sodium and increasing the intake of nutrient-rich foods that can help lower blood pressure. The daily recommended consumption of sodium on a Dash diet is between 1,500 to 2,300 milligrams versus the usual consumption of 9,000 to 12,000 milligrams.

The potassium, calcium, magnesium, protein, and fiber in the food help stabilize the blood pressure, that is why foods rich in these minerals and nutrients take the center stage in the Dash diet.

Benefits of Dash Diet

Apart from keeping the blood pressure at a normal level, the Dash diet also has other wonderful health benefits in preventing diabetes, cancer, heart disease, stroke, metabolic syndrome, and other deadly diseases. The vitamins and minerals from the type of foods included in the Dash diet can balance other nutrients, improve insulin resistance, promote weight loss, and offer long-term protection against illnesses.

Since it promotes healthy eating, anybody can try and enjoy the benefits of the Dash diet even if they do not have high blood pressure. It is important to note that sodium plays an important role in the normal functioning of the body and totally eliminating it from our diets can be harmful. The Dash diet encourages a healthy balance of nutritious foods and only a reduction of our salt intake.

Foods to Eat

The Dash diet recommends eating lots of fruits and vegetables, low-fat dairy products, and whole grains. Fish, poultry, legumes, seeds, and nuts are also encouraged in moderate amounts. Highly processed foods often contain high amounts of sodium and should therefore be avoided. Likewise, sugary drinks and eating foods high in sugar are also discouraged.

Below are some examples of the foods you can eat on a Dash diet.

- Vegetables – Spinach, collard greens, kale, arugula, Swiss chard, romaine lettuce, carrot, sweet potatoes, bell peppers, and red beets.
- Fruits – Berries, banana, avocado, tomato, cantaloupe, watermelon, kiwi, and pomegranates.
- Low-fat dairy –Low-fat or skimmed milk, natural and unsweetened yogurt, mozzarella, and cottage cheese.
- Herbs and spices – Garlic, onion, ginger, black pepper, basil, rosemary, thyme, parsley, cilantro, and cinnamon.
- Lean meat and Fish – Chicken, turkey, salmon, mackerel, herring, oyster, sardine, anchovies, and seabass.

Tips for Getting Started

Each of us has different dietary requirements. If you have any existing medical conditions, don't hesitate to talk to your doctor or dietician before making big changes to your diet.

If you have been constantly experiencing high blood pressure, here are some tips you can follow to get you started with the Dash diet.

- One of the first things you can do is to know what type of foods to eat and to avoid. Your dietician can guide you with the portion sizes and the type of foods you can combine.
- Learn how to read the nutrition facts label of products to know how much sodium they contain.
- Look for unsalted versions of canned goods such as tuna, vegetables, and peas. You may also rinse them with water to wash away excess sodium.
- Opt for salt alternatives to use for cooking. Look for potassium chloride salts or sodium-free spice and herb blends as seasoning.
- Whenever possible, aim to prepare your own meals at home so you know exactly what goes into it.
- Add one serving of vegetables to at least two of your daily meals until you can eat up to five servings per day.
- Aim to get a good variety of foods to get optimum nutrients. Let vegetables take the greater portion of your meals and lean meat only as a small part.
- Frozen vegetables are a great option since you can store them longer, but make sure that you also eat fresh vegetables regularly.
- Gradually substitute refined products with whole wheat, whole oats, brown rice, buckwheat, oatmeal, and quinoa.
- Instead of snacking on crackers and sweets, eat a serving of fresh fruit when you get hungry. You may also substitute them for dessert or mix them with your unsweetened yogurt.
- Keep unsalted nuts and seeds as a snack to keep you from reaching for unhealthy foods in between meals.
- Limit your consumption of red meat and opt for protein-rich vegetables like spinach, broccoli, beans, peas, Brussels sprouts, and mushrooms.
- Use healthier oils like olive, canola, soybean, safflower, peanut, corn, almond, and

sunflower when cooking or making salads.
- Try replacing some of your meals with vegetarian or vegan dishes.
- Eliminate sugary drinks, sodas, and high-sugar foods in your diet and replace them with fresh fruits and smoothies.

Chapter 2: 30-Day Meal Plan

Day 1

Breakfast: Crispy frittata

Lunch: Spicy green beans

Dinner: General Tso's chicken

Day 2

Breakfast: Breakfast peppers

Lunch: Crispy green tomatoes

Dinner: Sesame cod & snap peas

Day 3

Breakfast: Broccoli & cheese quiche

Lunch: Onion rings

Dinner: Salmon with horseradish rub

Day 4

Breakfast: Hash browns

Lunch: Coconut shrimp

Dinner: Salmon cakes with spicy mayo

Day 5

Breakfast: Egg tarts

Lunch: Roasted vegetables

Dinner: Garlic & rosemary lamb chops

Day 6

Breakfast: Breakfast biscuits

Lunch: Buttermilk fried chicken

Dinner: Garlic popcorn shrimp

Day 7

Breakfast: Breakfast sausage

Lunch: Chicken & broccoli

Dinner: Meatballs

Day 8

Breakfast: Breakfast sausage

Lunch: Crunchy chicken tenderloins

Dinner: Juicy steaks

Day 9

Breakfast: Flaxseed French toast with strawberries

Lunch: Korean fried chicken

Dinner: Sesame cod & snap peas

Day 10

Breakfast: Breakfast peppers

Lunch: Crispy fish

Dinner: Mustard pork tenderloin

Day 11

Breakfast: Broccoli & cheese quiche

Lunch: Roasted okra

Dinner: Garlic popcorn shrimp

Day 12

Breakfast: Breakfast casserole

Lunch: Brussels sprouts with bacon

Dinner: Lemon chicken

Day 13

Breakfast: Hash Browns

Lunch: Crispy chicken breast

Dinner: Falafel

Day 14

Breakfast: Breakfast stuffed pastries

Lunch: Baked potatoes with broccoli

Dinner: Ranch pork chops

Day 15

Breakfast: Egg tarts

Lunch: Coconut shrimp

Dinner: Rib eye steak

Day 16

Breakfast: Breakfast biscuits

Lunch: Scallops with lemon herb sauce

Dinner: General Tso's chicken

Day 17

Breakfast: Flaxseed French toast with strawberries

Lunch: Salmon with horseradish rub

Dinner: Chicken & broccoli

Day 18

Breakfast: Breakfast peppers

Lunch: Crispy fish

Dinner: Meatballs

Day 19

Breakfast: Crispy frittata

Lunch: Fish cakes

Dinner: Lamb chops with mustard & garlic

Day 20

Breakfast: Broccoli & cheese quiche

Lunch: Crispy chicken breast

Dinner: Juicy steaks

Day 21

Breakfast: Breakfast casserole

Lunch: Sausages

Dinner: Roasted vegetables

Day 22

Breakfast: Breakfast stuffed pastries

Lunch: Brussels sprouts with bacon

Dinner: Calamari

Day 23

Breakfast: Breakfast sausage

Lunch: Salmon cakes with spicy mayo

Dinner: Mexican chicken wings

Day 24

Breakfast: Egg tarts

Lunch: Onion rings

Dinner: Lemon paprika shrimp

Day 25

Breakfast: Breakfast biscuits

Lunch: Baked potatoes

Dinner: Roast beef

Day 26

Breakfast: Crispy frittata

Lunch: Garlic & rosemary lamb chops

Dinner: Crunchy chicken tenderloins

Day 27

Breakfast: Breakfast casserole

Lunch: Ranch pork chops

Dinner: Eggplant parmesan

Day 28

Breakfast: Flaxseed French toast with strawberries

Lunch: Pork chop & Brussels sprouts

Dinner: Sausages

Day 29

Breakfast: Hash Browns

Lunch: Calamari

Dinner: Roast chicken

Day 30

Breakfast: Breakfast stuffed pastries

Lunch: Mexican chicken wings

Dinner: Lamb chops with mustard & garlic

Chapter 3: Breakfast Recipes

Cheesy Frittata

Preparation Time: 10 minutes
Cooking Time: 20 minutes
Servings: 4

Ingredients:

- 4 eggs, beaten
- 1 green onion, chopped
- 2 tablespoons red bell pepper, diced
- ½ cup cheddar, shredded
- ¼ lb. low-sodium breakfast sausage, cooked, removed from casing and crumbled
- Pinch cayenne pepper
- Cooking spray

Method:

1. Mix all the ingredients in a bowl.
2. Preheat your air fryer to 360 degrees F.
3. Spray a small cake pan with oil.
4. Pour mixture into the pan.
5. Air fry for 20 minutes.

Serving Suggestions: Garnish with chopped parsley.

Preparation & Cooking Tips: Omit cayenne pepper if you don't want your frittata spicy.

Breakfast Biscuits

Preparation Time: 15 minutes
Cooking Time: 10 minutes
Servings: 8

Ingredients:

- 2 eggs, beaten and cooked
- 4 slices turkey bacon, cooked crisp and crumbled
- 2 oz. cheddar cheese, sliced into cubes
- Pepper to taste
- 10 oz. refrigerated biscuits
- 1 egg, beaten
- 1 tablespoon water

Method:

1. In a bowl, mix the eggs, bacon, cheese and pepper.
2. Separate the refrigerate dough into 5.
3. Separate each biscuit into 2.
4. Press the biscuits to form a round shape.
5. Top with the egg mixture.
6. Place another biscuit on top and seal the edges.
7. Mix remaining egg and water.
8. Brush biscuits with this mixture.
9. Cook in the air fryer at 325 degrees F for 10 minutes.

Serving Suggestions: Serve with coffee and milk.

Preparation & Cooking Tips: You can also use pepper Jack cheese for this recipe.

Flaxseed French Toast with Strawberries

Preparation Time: 15 minutes
Cooking Time: 10 minutes
Servings: 4

Ingredients:

- ¼ cup brown sugar, divided
- ½ teaspoon ground cinnamon
- 2 eggs, beaten
- 1 teaspoon vanilla extract
- ¼ cup nonfat milk
- 4 slices whole-grain bread, sliced into strips
- 2/3 cup flax seed meal
- Cooking spray
- 1 teaspoon powdered sugar
- 2 cups strawberries, sliced

Method:

1. Add 1 tablespoon brown sugar to a bowl.
2. Stir in the cinnamon, eggs, vanilla and milk.
3. Dip the bread strips into the mixture.
4. Dredge with the flax seed meal and spray with oil.
5. Air fry at 375 degrees F for 10 minutes, turning once.
6. Add to a serving plate.
7. Sprinkle with powdered sugar.
8. Serve with strawberries on the side.

Serving Suggestions: Drizzle with honey or maple syrup.

Preparation & Cooking Tips: Choose a high-quality whole grain loaf for this recipe

Hash Browns

Preparation Time: 45 minutes
Cooking Time: 20 minutes
Servings: 8

Ingredients:

- 2 teaspoons vegetable oil, divided
- 4 potatoes, grated
- 2 tablespoons corn flour
- Salt and pepper to taste
- 2 teaspoons red pepper flakes

Method:

1. Add half of oil to a pan over medium heat.
2. Cook the grated potatoes for 5 minutes, stirring often.
3. Transfer to a plate and let cool.
4. Stir in the rest of the ingredients.
5. Form patties from the mixture.
6. Refrigerate for 30 minutes.
7. Cook in the air fryer at 350 degrees F for 15 minutes, turning once.

Serving Suggestions: Serve with ketchup and mayo.

Preparation & Cooking Tips: Soak grated potatoes for 1 hour and dry thoroughly before cooking.

Breakfast Sausage

Preparation Time: 5 minutes
Cooking Time: 10 minutes
Servings: 4

Ingredients:

- 12 oz. low-fat, low-sodium sausage patties
- Cooking spray

Method:

1. Preheat your air fryer to 400 degrees F.
2. Add sausage patties to the air fryer basket.
3. Spray with oil.
4. Air fry for 5 minutes per side.

Serving Suggestions: Serve with hash browns and green salad.

Preparation & Cooking Tips: Cook in batches.

Egg Tarts

Preparation Time: 5 minutes
Cooking Time: 20 minutes
Servings: 2

Ingredients:

- 17 oz. frozen puff pastry, sliced into 4 squares
- ¾ cup Monterey Jack cheese, shredded
- 4 eggs

Method:

1. Air fry the puff pastry at 390 degrees F for 10 minutes.
2. Press the middle part of the sheet to make indentation.
3. Sprinkle with cheese and crack eggs on top.
4. Air fry for 10 minutes.

Serving Suggestions: Sprinkle with chopped parsley.

Preparation & Cooking Tips: You can also use gruyere cheese for this recipe.

Breakfast Casserole

Preparation Time: 10 minutes
Cooking Time: 25 minutes
Servings: 8

Ingredients:

- 1 teaspoon olive oil
- 1 lb. ground turkey sausage
- 1 green bell pepper, diced
- ¼ cup white onion, diced
- 8 eggs, beaten
- ½ cup Colby Jack cheese, shredded
- 1 teaspoon fennel seed
- Garlic salt to taste

Method:

1. Add oil to a pan over medium heat.
2. Cook sausage, bell pepper and onion for 10 minutes, stirring often.
3. Transfer to a bowl.
4. Stir in the remaining ingredients.
5. Transfer to a small baking pan.
6. Add to the air fryer basket.
7. Air fry at 390 degrees F for 15 minutes.

Serving Suggestions: Sprinkle with chopped green onion.

Preparation & Cooking Tips: You can also use low-sodium lean ground pork sausage.

Breakfast Peppers

Preparation Time: 10 minutes
Cooking Time: 15 minutes
Servings: 2

Ingredients:

- 2 red or green bell peppers, seeded and sliced in half
- 1 teaspoon olive oil
- 4 eggs
- Salt and pepper to taste

Method:

1. Brush the bell pepper halves with oil.
2. Crack eggs into the bell pepper halves.
3. Season with salt and pepper.
4. Add to the air fryer.
5. Cook at 330 degrees F for 15 minutes.

Serving Suggestions: Sprinkle with sriracha flakes.

Preparation & Cooking Tips: Use large bell peppers for this recipe.

Breakfast Stuffed Pastries

Preparation Time: 15 minutes
Cooking Time: 15 minutes
Servings: 4

Ingredients:

- 1 box puff pastry sheets, sliced into rectangles
- 5 eggs, beaten
- ½ cup turkey sausage, cooked and crumbled
- ½ cup cheddar cheese, shredded
- Cooking spray

Method:

1. Cook the eggs in a pan over medium heat.
2. Transfer to a bowl.
3. Stir in turkey sausage.
4. Top pastry sheets with egg mixture.
5. Top with cheese.
6. Add another pastry sheet on top.
7. Press to seal edges.
8. Spray with oil.
9. Air fry at 370 degrees F for 10 minutes.

Serving Suggestions: Serve with milk or coffee.

Preparation & Cooking Tips: You can also add chopped ham to the egg mixture.

Broccoli & Cheese Quiche

Preparation Time: 20 minutes
Cooking Time: 20 minutes
Servings: 2

Ingredients:

- 2 eggs, beaten
- 1 cup low-fat milk
- 2 cups broccoli florets, steamed
- 1 cup cheddar cheese, grated
- 1 tomato, chopped
- 1 teaspoon dried thyme
- 1 teaspoon parsley, chopped
- Salt and pepper to taste

Method:

1. Combine all the ingredients in a bowl.
2. Mix well.
3. Transfer to a small baking pan.
4. Place the pan in the air fryer.
5. Cook in the air fryer at 360 degrees F for 20 minutes.

Serving Suggestions: Top with crumbled feta cheese.

Preparation & Cooking Tips: You can also use nondairy milk for this recipe.

Chapter 4: Chicken Recipes

Crispy Chicken Breast

Preparation Time: 15 minutes
Cooking Time: 15 minutes
Servings: 2

Ingredients:

- 1 egg, beaten
- ¼ cup all-purpose flour
- ¾ cup breadcrumbs
- 1 teaspoon dried oregano
- 2 teaspoon lemon zest
- ¼ cup Parmesan cheese, grated
- Salt and pepper to taste
- ½ teaspoon cayenne pepper
- 2 chicken breast fillets

Method:

1. Add the eggs to a bowl.
2. Add the flour to another bowl.
3. In the third bowl, mix the breadcrumbs, dried oregano, lemon zest, Parmesan cheese, salt, pepper and cayenne pepper.
4. Dip the chicken breast fillets in the first, second and third bowls.
5. Add these to the air fryer basket.
6. Cook at 375 degrees F for 10 minutes.
7. Turn the chicken.
8. Cook for another 5 minutes.

Serving Suggestions: Serve with light mayo and ketchup.

Preparation & Cooking Tips: Cook for a few minutes more if you want your chicken crispier.

Chicken & Broccoli

Preparation Time: 10 minutes
Cooking Time: 20 minutes
Servings: 4

Ingredients:

- 1 onion, sliced
- 2 cups broccoli florets
- 1 lb. chicken breast fillet, sliced into cubes
- 2 tablespoons olive oil
- ½ teaspoon garlic powder
- 1 tablespoon ginger, minced
- 1 tablespoon reduced-sodium soy sauce
- 1 teaspoon sesame seed oil
- 2 teaspoons rice vinegar

Method:

1. Toss the onion, broccoli and chicken in a bowl.
2. In another bowl, m ix the rest of the ingredients.
3. Pour mixture into the first bowl.
4. Mix well.
5. Add mixture to the air fryer.
6. Cook at 380 degrees F for 20 minutes.

Serving Suggestions: Drizzle with lemon juice before serving.

Preparation & Cooking Tips: You can also use cauliflower florets for this recipe.

Mexican Chicken Wings

Preparation Time: 10 minutes
Cooking Time: 12 minutes
Servings: 5

Ingredients:

- 3 lb. chicken wings
- 2 teaspoons olive oil
- 1 tablespoon taco seasoning mix

Method:

1. Coat chicken wings with olive oil.
2. Sprinkle all sides with taco seasoning.
3. Preheat your air fryer to 350 degrees F.
4. Add the chicken wings to the air fryer.
5. Cook for 6 minutes per side.

Serving Suggestions: Serve with salsa and sour cream.

Preparation & Cooking Tips: You can also use chicken thighs or legs for this recipe.

Crunchy Chicken Tenderloins

Preparation Time: 10 minutes
Cooking Time: 15 minutes
Servings: 4

Ingredients:

- 1 egg, beaten
- 2 tablespoons vegetable oil
- ½ cup breadcrumbs
- 8 chicken tenderloins

Method:

1. Preheat your air fryer to 350 degrees F.
2. Add the egg to a bowl.
3. Mix the oil and breadcrumbs in another bowl.
4. Dip the chicken in egg and then in the oil mixture.
5. Add to the air fryer basket.
6. Cook for 15 minutes, flipping once or twice.

Serving Suggestions: Serve with ranch dip.

Preparation & Cooking Tips: You can also use chicken breast strips for this recipe.

General Tso's Chicken

Preparation Time: 20 minutes
Cooking Time: 35 minutes
Servings: 4

Ingredients:

- 1 lb. chicken thigh fillets, sliced into smaller pieces
- Salt and pepper to taste
- 1 egg, beaten
- ¼ cup cornstarch

Sauce

- 2 tablespoons reduced sodium soy sauce
- 1 ½ tablespoons vegetable oil
- 2 teaspoons rice vinegar
- 8 tablespoons chicken broth
- 2 teaspoons sugar
- 2 tablespoons ketchup
- 3 chiles de árbol, chopped and seeded
- 1 clove garlic, minced
- 1 tablespoon ginger, chopped

Method:

1. Season chicken with salt and pepper.
2. Dip in egg and coat with cornstarch.
3. Air fry at 400 degrees F for 15 minutes, flipping once or twice.
4. In a pan over medium heat, simmer sauce ingredients for 15 minutes.
5. Add chicken to the pan.
6. Mix well.

7. Cook for 5 minutes.
8. Serve warm.

Serving Suggestions: Garnish with sesame seeds and chopped green onions.

Preparation & Cooking Tips: You can also use chicken breast fillet for this recipe.

Roast Chicken

Preparation Time: 10 minutes
Cooking Time: 50 minutes
Servings: 8

Ingredients:

- 1 whole chicken
- Chicken dry rub
- Cooking spray

Method:

1. Spray chicken with oil.
2. Sprinkle with the dry rub.
3. Roast in the air fryer at 330 degrees F for 30 minutes.
4. Turn and roast for another 20 minutes.

Serving Suggestions: Serve with mashed potatoes and gravy.

Preparation & Cooking Tips: You can also use whole turkey for this recipe.

Korean Fried Chicken

Preparation Time: 15 minutes
Cooking Time: 30 minutes
Servings: 1

Ingredients:

- 1 lb. chicken wings
- 1 tablespoon oil
- Salt and pepper to taste
- 3 tablespoons cornstarch

Sauce

- ½ tablespoon reduced-sodium soy sauce
- ½ tablespoon toasted sesame oil
- 1 tablespoon Korean chili garlic paste
- 1 tablespoon honey
- 1 tablespoon ketchup
- 1 tablespoon brown sugar
- 2 cloves garlic, minced
- ½ tablespoon ginger, grated

Method:

1. Brush chicken wings with oil.
2. Season with salt and pepper.
3. Coat with cornstarch.
4. Air fry at 400 degrees F for 15 minutes.
5. Mix sauce ingredients in a pan over medium heat.
6. Bring to a boil.
7. Reduce heat and simmer for 10 minutes.

8. Toss chicken wings in the sauce and serve.

Serving Suggestions: Garnish with white sesame seeds.

Preparation & Cooking Tips: Korean chili paste is available in most Asian stores.

Buttermilk Fried Chicken

Preparation Time: 8 hours and 20 minutes
Cooking Time: 45 minutes
Servings: 6

Ingredients:

Marinade

- 2 lb. chicken
- 1 cup buttermilk
- ¼ cup hot sauce
- 1 teaspoon paprika
- 1 teaspoon garlic powder
- Salt and pepper to taste

Breading

- 1 cup flour
- 1 teaspoon garlic powder
- 1 teaspoon paprika
- ½ cup cornstarch
- Salt and pepper to taste
- Cooking spray

Method:

1. Mix the marinade ingredients in a bowl.
2. Cover and refrigerate for 8 hours.
3. Preheat your air fryer to 375 degrees F.
4. In a bowl, mix the breading ingredients.
5. Add 2 tablespoons buttermilk batter to the flour bowl and mix well.
6. Dredge chicken with flour mixture.

7. Cook the chicken for 30 minutes.
8. Flip and cook for 15 minutes.

Serving Suggestions: Serve with mayo and ketchup.

Preparation & Cooking Tips: Use chicken thighs and legs for this recipe.

Parmesan Chicken

Preparation Time: 10 minutes
Cooking Time: 15 minutes
Servings: 2

Ingredients:

- 2 eggs, beaten
- 2 teaspoons paprika
- 1 ½ cups Parmesan cheese, grated
- 2 tablespoons garlic paste
- 2 tablespoons dried Italian seasoning
- 2 chicken breast fillets, sliced in half
- Salt to taste
- Cooking spray

Method:

1. Preheat your air fryer to 400 degrees F.
2. Combine paprika, cheese, garlic paste and Italian seasoning in a bowl.
3. Add the eggs to a bowl.
4. Season chicken with salt.
5. Dip in egg and then in paprika mixture.
6. Spray with oil.
7. Air fry for 15 minutes.

Serving Suggestions: Serve with roasted vegetables.

Preparation & Cooking Tips: You can also use chicken thigh fillets for this recipe.

Lemon Chicken

Preparation Time: 10 minutes
Cooking Time: 20 minutes
Servings: 4

Ingredients:

- 6 chicken thighs
- 2 tablespoons olive oil
- 2 tablespoons lemon juice
- 1 tablespoon Italian herb seasoning blend
- Salt and pepper to taste
- 4 lemon slices for garnish

Method:

1. Combine ingredients except garnish in a bowl.
2. Marinate for 30 minutes.
3. Place chicken in the air fryer basket.
4. Top with lemon slices.
5. Cook at 350 degrees F for 10 minutes per side.

Serving Suggestions: Drizzle with lemon juice before serving.

Preparation & Cooking Tips: You can also use chicken fillet for this recipe.

Chapter 5: Meat Recipes

Rib Eye Steak

Preparation Time: 2 hours and 10 minutes
Cooking Time: 16 minutes
Servings: 2

Ingredients:

- 2 tablespoons olive oil
- ½ cup low-sodium soy sauce
- 4 teaspoons steak seasoning
- 2 rib-eye steaks, fat trimmed

Method:

1. Mix olive oil, soy sauce and steak seasoning in a bowl.
2. Add the steaks.
3. Turn to coat evenly.
4. Cover and marinate in the refrigerator for 2 hours.
5. Preheat your air fryer to 400 degrees F.
6. Air fry the steaks for 8 minutes per side.

Serving Suggestions: Let rest for 5 minutes before serving. Serve with green salad.

Preparation & Cooking Tips: Choose a cut that's one and a half inch thick.

Mustard Pork Tenderloin

Preparation Time: 4 hours and 10 minutes
Cooking Time: 20 minutes
Servings: 4

Ingredients:

- 2 tablespoons brown sugar
- ¼ cup Dijon mustard
- ½ teaspoon dried thyme
- 1 teaspoon dried parsley
- Salt and pepper to taste
- 1 ¼ lb. pork tenderloin

Method:

1. Combine all the ingredients in a bowl.
2. Cover and marinate in the refrigerator for 4 hours.
3. Preheat your air fryer to 400 degrees F.
4. Air fry the pork for 20 minutes.

Serving Suggestions: Serve with roasted green beans or potatoes.

Preparation & Cooking Tips: You can also marinate the night before.

Ranch Pork Chops

Preparation Time: 20 minutes
Cooking Time: 10 minutes
Servings: 4

Ingredients:

- 4 pork chops
- Cooking spray
- Garlic salt to taste
- 1 teaspoon ranch dressing mix
- Sour cream

Method:

1. Spray both sides of the pork chops with oil.
2. Sprinkle with the garlic salt and ranch dressing mix.
3. Marinate for 10 minutes.
4. Cook in the air fryer at 390 degrees F for 5 minutes per side.
5. Serve with sour cream.

Serving Suggestions: Let rest for 5 minutes before serving.

Preparation & Cooking Tips: For thicker cut pork chops, add 3 to 5 minutes of cooking time.

Lamb Chops with Mustard & Garlic

Preparation Time: 45 minutes

Cooking Time: 20 minutes

Servings: 2

Ingredients:

Marinade

- 1 teaspoon garlic, minced
- 2 teaspoons olive oil
- 2 teaspoons Dijon mustard
- 1 teaspoon soy sauce
- 1 teaspoon cayenne pepper
- 1 teaspoon cumin powder
- Salt to taste

Lamb

- 8 lamb chops

Method:

1. Combine the marinade ingredients in a bowl.
2. Add the lamb chops.
3. Cover and marinate for 30 minutes.
4. Add to the air fryer basket.
5. Air fry at 350 degrees F for 20 minutes, flipping once or twice.

Serving Suggestions: Sprinkle with cumin before serving.

Preparation & Cooking Tips: For thicker lamb chops, add 3 to 5 minutes of cooking time.

Garlic & Rosemary Lamb Chops

Preparation Time: 10 minutes
Cooking Time: 15 minutes
Servings: 2

Ingredients:

- 4 lamb chops
- 2 teaspoons olive oil
- Salt and pepper to taste
- 1 clove garlic, minced
- 2 tablespoons rosemary, chopped

Method:

1. Brush lamb chops with oil.
2. Season with salt and pepper.
3. Place in the air fryer basket.
4. Top with garlic and rosemary.
5. Cook at 360 degrees F and cook for 6 to 8 minutes per side.

Serving Suggestions: Garnish with lemon wedges.

Preparation & Cooking Tips: You can also let lamb chops marinate in the garlic and rosemary for 30 minutes.

Meatballs

Preparation Time: 20 minutes
Cooking Time: 10 minutes
Servings: 8

Ingredients:

- 16 oz. lean ground beef
- 4 oz. lean ground pork
- 1 egg, beaten
- 2 cloves garlic, minced
- ¼ cup breadcrumbs
- ½ cup Parmesan cheese, grated
- 1 teaspoon Italian seasoning
- Salt to taste

Method:

1. Preheat your air fryer to 350 degrees F.
2. Mix all the ingredients in a bowl.
3. Form meatballs from the mixture.
4. Add meatballs to the air fryer.
5. Cook for 8 minutes.
6. Shake and cook for another 2 minutes.

Serving Suggestions: Serve with marinara sauce.

Preparation & Cooking Tips: Make the meatballs ahead of time by mixing the above ingredients and freezing the meatballs for up to 1 month. Add 15 more minutes to the cooking time.

Sausages

Preparation Time: 5 minutes

Cooking Time: 10 minutes

Servings: 4

Ingredients:

- Poke the sausages in 3 places each with a sharp knife, breaking through the casing.
- Arrange the sausages in a single non-overlapping layer in the air fryer.

Method:

1. Add the sausages to the air fryer.
2. Air fry at 400 degrees F for 12 minutes.

Serving Suggestions: Serve with hot sauce and mustard.

Preparation & Cooking Tips: Poke the sausages with a fork before cooking.

Juicy Steaks

Preparation Time: 20 minutes
Cooking Time: 12 minutes
Servings: 2

Ingredients:

- 2 rib eye steaks
- Salt and pepper to taste
- 2 tablespoons olive oil

Garlic butter sauce

- ½ cup butter (unsalted), softened
- 1 teaspoon Worcestershire Sauce
- 2 teaspoons garlic, minced
- 2 tablespoons parsley, chopped
- Salt to taste

Method:

1. Combine the garlic butter sauce ingredients in a bowl.
2. Form a log from the mixture.
3. Wrap with foil and refrigerate.
4. Coat steaks with olive oil.
5. Sprinkle both sides with salt and pepper.
6. Cook in the air fryer at 400 degrees F for 6 minutes per side.
7. Add garlic butter on top.

Serving Suggestions: Serve with green salad.

Preparation & Cooking Tips: Let steaks rest for 20 minutes before coating with olive oil and seasoning.

Roast Beef

Preparation Time: 15 minutes
Cooking Time: 45 minutes
Servings: 6

Ingredients:

- 1 tablespoons olive oil
- 1 teaspoon thyme
- 1 teaspoon rosemary
- Salt to taste
- 2 lb. beef roast

Method:

1. Preheat your air fryer to 390 degrees F.
2. Combine olive oil, thyme, rosemary and salt in a dish.
3. Rub mixture all over the beef roast.
4. Add beef roast to the air fryer basket.
5. Cook at 360 degrees F for 15 minutes.
6. Reduce heat to 340 degrees F and cook for another 30 minutes.

Serving Suggestions: Serve with roasted vegetables.

Preparation & Cooking Tips: You can also make slits on the beef roast and insert garlic slivers.

Pork Chops & Brussels Sprouts

Preparation Time: 15 minutes
Cooking Time: 15 minutes
Servings: 2

Ingredients:

- 2 pork chops
- Cooking spray
- Salt and pepper to taste
- 2 teaspoons olive oil
- 2 cups Brussels sprouts
- 1 teaspoon mustard
- 2 teaspoons maple syrup

Method:

1. Spray both sides of pork chops with oil.
2. Season with salt and pepper.
3. In a bowl, mix the remaining ingredients.
4. Add the pork chops to one side of the air fryer.
5. Place the Brussels sprouts on the other side.
6. Cook at 400 degrees F for 15 minutes.

Serving Suggestions: Drizzle with maple syrup before serving.

Preparation & Cooking Tips: If available, use Dijon mustard for this recipe.

Chapter 6: Fish & Seafood Recipes

Sesame Cod & Snap Peas

Preparation Time: 10 minutes
Cooking Time: 20 minutes
Servings: 4

Ingredients:

- Cooking spray
- 4 cod fillets
- Salt and pepper to taste
- 3 tablespoons butter, melted
- 2 tablespoons sesame seeds
- Vegetable oil
- 3 cloves garlic, sliced thinly
- 12 oz. sugar snap peas
- 1 orange, sliced into wedges

Method:

1. Preheat it to 400 degrees F.
2. Sprinkle both sides of fish with salt and pepper.
3. In a bowl, mix sesame seeds and butter.
4. Reserve 2 tablespoons of this mixture.
5. Toss garlic and peas in the butter mixture.
6. Air fry for 10 minutes, shaking once.
7. Brush both sides of fish with reserved butter mixture.
8. Cook for 5 minutes per side.
9. Serve fish with snap peas and garlic.

Serving Suggestions: Garnish with orange wedges.

Preparation & Cooking Tips: You can also toast sesame seeds first before mixing with butter.

Coconut Shrimp

Preparation Time: 10 minutes
Cooking Time: 6 minutes
Servings: 6

Ingredients:

- Pepper to taste
- ½ cup all-purpose flour
- 2 eggs
- ¼ cup breadcrumbs
- ⅔ cup coconut flakes (unsweetened)
- 12 oz. shrimp, peeled and deveined
- Cooking spray
- Salt to taste
- ¼ cup lime juice
- ¼ cup honey
- 1 Serrano chili, chopped

Method:

1. Mix pepper and flour in a bowl.
2. Add the eggs to another bowl.
3. In a third bowl, combine breadcrumbs and coconut flakes.
4. Coat shrimp with flour.
5. Dip in eggs and dredge with breadcrumbs.
6. Spray with oil.
7. Cook in the air fryer for 3 minutes per side.
8. Season with salt.
9. In a bowl, mix the remaining ingredients.
10. Serve shrimp with lime honey dip.

Serving Suggestions: Garnish with chopped cilantro.

Preparation & Cooking Tips: Replace Serrano chili with 2 teaspoons red pepper flakes if not available.

Fish Cakes

Preparation Time: 10 minutes
Cooking Time: 20 minutes
Servings: 2

Ingredients:

- Cooking spray
- 10 oz. cod fillet, chopped
- 3 tablespoons cilantro, chopped
- ¼ cup breadcrumbs
- ¼ cup breadcrumbs
- 1 egg, beaten
- 2 tablespoons light mayonnaise
- 2 tablespoons Thai sweet chili sauce
- Salt and pepper to taste

Method:

1. Spray air fryer basket with oil.
2. Combine all ingredients in a bowl.
3. Form patties from the mixture.
4. Spray patties with oil.
5. Add to the air fryer basket.
6. Air fry at 400 degrees F for 10 minutes, flipping once.

Serving Suggestions: Garnish with chopped cilantro.

Preparation & Cooking Tips: Make fish cakes ahead of time by freezing the mixture and air frying the frozen fish cakes when ready to serve.

Lemon Paprika Shrimp

Preparation Time: 10 minutes
Cooking Time: 10 minutes
Servings: 2

Ingredients:

- 1 tablespoon olive oil
- 1 tablespoon lemon juice
- 1 teaspoon lemon pepper
- ¼ teaspoon paprika
- ¼ teaspoon garlic powder
- 12 Oz. shrimp, peeled and deveined

Method:

1. Preheat your air fryer to 400 degrees F.
2. Combine all the ingredients in a bowl.
3. Coat shrimp evenly with the sauce mixture.
4. Add shrimp to the air fryer.
5. Cook for 8 to 10 minutes.

Serving Suggestions: Garnish with lemon slices.

Preparation & Cooking Tips: You can also use frozen peeled shrimp.

Crispy Fish

Preparation Time: 10 minutes
Cooking Time: 15 minutes
Servings: 4

Ingredients:

- ¼ cup vegetable oil
- 1 cup breadcrumbs
- 4 flounder fillets
- 1 egg, beaten

Method:

1. Preheat your air fryer to 350 degrees F.
2. Combine oil and breadcrumbs in a bowl.
3. Soak the fish in the egg.
4. Coat with the breadcrumb mixture.
5. Add to the air fryer basket.
6. Air fry for 15 minutes, turning once.

Serving Suggestions: Garnish with lemon slices.

Preparation & Cooking Tips: You can also use other white fish fillet for this recipe.

Salmon with Horseradish Rub

Preparation Time: 10 minutes

Cooking Time: 15 minutes

Servings: 2

Ingredients:

- Cooking spray
- 1 tablespoon olive oil
- 2 tablespoons horseradish, grated
- 1 tablespoon capers, chopped
- 1 tablespoon parsley, chopped
- 2 salmon fillets
- Salt and pepper to taste

Method:

1. Spray your air fryer basket with oil.
2. Mix oil, horseradish, capers and parsley in a bowl.
3. Season salmon with salt and pepper.
4. Spread horseradish mixture on top of salmon.
5. Air fry at 375 degrees F for 15 minutes.

Serving Suggestions: Let rest for 5 minutes before serving.

Preparation & Cooking Tips: Spray salmon with oil after spreading it with horseradish mixture.

Garlic Popcorn Shrimp

Preparation Time: 15 minutes
Cooking Time: 8 minutes
Servings: 4

Ingredients:

- Cooking spray
- ½ cup all-purpose flour
- 2 tablespoons water
- 2 eggs, beaten
- 1 tablespoon garlic powder
- 1 tablespoon ground cumin
- 1 ½ cups breadcrumbs
- 1 lb. shrimp, peeled and deveined

Dipping sauce

- ½ cup ketchup
- 2 tablespoons lime juice
- 2 tablespoons fresh cilantro leaves, chopped
- 2 tablespoons chipotle chili in adobo, chopped
- Salt to taste

Method:

1. Spray your air fryer basket with oil.
2. Add flour to a dish.
3. In a bowl, mix water and eggs.
4. In another bowl, combine garlic powder, cumin and breadcrumbs.
5. Coat shrimp with flour.
6. Dip shrimp in egg and dredge with garlic powder mixture.

7. Spray with oil.
8. Air fry at 360 degrees F for 8 minutes, flipping once.
9. Mix the remaining ingredients.
10. Serve shrimp with dipping sauce.

Serving Suggestions: Garnish with lime wedges.

Preparation & Cooking Tips: Use freshly squeezed lime juice.

Calamari

Preparation Time: 10 minutes
Cooking Time: 4 minutes
Servings: 4

Ingredients:

- ½ cup all-purpose flour
- 1 egg
- ¼ cup milk
- Salt and pepper to taste
- 2 cups breadcrumbs
- 1 lb. calamari rings
- Cooking spray

Method:

1. Preheat your air fryer to 400 degrees F.
2. Add flour to a bowl.
3. Beat egg and milk in another bowl.
4. Mix salt, pepper and breadcrumbs in a third bowl.
5. Coat calamari with flour.
6. Dip in egg.
7. Dredge with breadcrumb mixture.
8. Air fry calamari for 4 minutes.
9. Flip and cook for another 3 minutes.

Serving Suggestions: Serve with cocktail sauce.

Preparation & Cooking Tips: Freeze breaded calamari and air fry when ready to cook.

Scallops with Lemon Herb Sauce

Preparation Time: 10 minutes
Cooking Time: 6 minutes
Servings: 2

Ingredients:

- Cooking spray
- 8 scallops
- Salt and pepper to taste
- ¼ cup olive oil
- ½ teaspoon garlic, chopped
- 1 teaspoon lemon zest
- 2 teaspoons capers, minced
- 2 tablespoons parsley, chopped

Method:

1. Spray your air fryer basket with oil.
2. Season scallops with salt and pepper.
3. Air fry scallops at 400 degrees F for 6 minutes.
4. In a bowl, mix the oil, garlic, lemon zest, capers and parsley.
5. Pour sauce over the scallops and serve.

Serving Suggestions: Garnish with lemon wedges.

Preparation & Cooking Tips: Dry scallops thoroughly before seasoning.

Salmon Cakes with Spicy Mayo

Preparation Time: 45 minutes

Cooking Time: 10 minutes

Servings: 4

Ingredients:

Spicy mayo

- ¼ cup mayonnaise
- 1 tablespoon hot sauce

Salmon cakes

- 1 lb. salmon fillets, chopped
- 1 egg, beaten
- ¼ cup almond flour
- 1 green onion, chopped
- 1 ½ teaspoon Old Bay seasoning
- Cooking spray

Method:

1. Mix spicy mayo ingredients.
2. Refrigerate until ready to use.
3. Combine salmon cake ingredients in a bowl.
4. Form patties from the mixture.
5. Refrigerate patties for 30 minutes.
6. Air fry the salmon cakes at 390 degrees F for 4 to 5 minutes per side.
7. Serve with spicy mayo mixture.

Serving Suggestions: Garnish with chopped green onion.

Preparation & Cooking Tips: Cook in batches.

Chapter 7: Vegetarian Recipes

Brussels Sprouts with Bacon

Preparation Time: 5 minutes
Cooking Time: 30 minutes
Servings: 8

Ingredients:

- 4 slices bacon
- 1 onion, chopped
- 3 lb. Brussels sprouts, sliced in half
- 1 tablespoon olive oil
- Salt and pepper to taste
- 2 teaspoons thyme
- 2 tablespoons lemon juice

Method:

1. Add bacon to the air fryer.
2. Air fry at 400 degrees F for 15 minutes, turning once.
3. Drain on a plate lined with paper towel.
4. Let cool and then crumble.
5. Coat onion and Brussels sprouts with oil.
6. Season with salt and pepper.
7. Cook in the air fryer at 375 degrees F for 15 minutes, shaking the basket once.
8. Top Brussels sprouts with bacon, thyme and lemon juice.

Serving Suggestions: Garnish with lemon wedges.

Preparation & Cooking Tips: Use center-cut bacon for this recipe if possible.

Baked Potatoes with Broccoli

Preparation Time: 15 minutes

Cooking Time: 25 minutes

Servings: 8

Ingredients:

- 4 potatoes
- 1 cup low-fat milk, divided
- 2 tablespoons all-purpose flour
- ½ cup Cheddar cheese, shredded and divided
- 1 cup broccoli florets, chopped
- Salt and pepper to taste

Method:

1. Poke potatoes with a fork.
2. Microwave on high for 10 minutes.
3. Transfer to a cutting board and slice in half.
4. In a pan over medium heat, simmer ¾ cup low-fat milk.
5. In a bowl, mix remaining milk and flour.
6. Add this to the pan.
7. Bring to a boil.
8. Turn off heat.
9. Add cheese, broccoli, salt and pepper to the pan.
10. Add the potatoes to the air fryer basket.
11. Top with the cheese mixture.
12. Air fry at 350 degrees F for 5 minutes.

Serving Suggestions: Garnish with chopped chives.

Preparation & Cooking Tips: You may also add a pinch of cayenne pepper to the mixture.

Roasted Vegetables

Preparation Time: 20 minutes
Cooking Time: 10 minutes
Servings: 4

Ingredients:

- 1 red bell pepper, sliced
- 1 squash, diced
- ½ cup zucchini, diced
- 1 cup cauliflower florets
- 1 cup mushrooms, diced
- 2 teaspoons vegetable oil
- Salt and pepper to taste

Method:

1. Preheat your air fryer to 360 degrees F.
2. Combine all the ingredients in a bowl.
3. Transfer to the air fryer basket.
4. Air fry for 10 minutes, shaking once or twice.

Serving Suggestions: Adjust seasoning before serving.

Preparation & Cooking Tips: You can also add other vegetables like carrots and potatoes.

Baked Potatoes

Preparation Time: 15 minutes

Cooking Time: 1 hour

Servings: 2

Ingredients:

- 2 potatoes
- 1 tablespoon peanut oil
- Salt to taste

Method:

1. Preheat your air fryer to 400 degrees F.
2. Coat potatoes with peanut oil.
3. Season with salt.
4. Add to the air fryer basket.
5. Air fry for 1 hour.

Serving Suggestions: Serve with sour cream or cheese sauce.

Preparation & Cooking Tips: Poke with a fork to see if the potatoes are done.

Falafel

Preparation Time: 10 minutes
Cooking Time: 12 minutes
Servings: 4

Ingredients:

- 1 cup chickpeas
- ¼ cup onion, chopped
- 2 cloves garlic, minced
- ½ cup parsley, chopped
- 1 tablespoon olive oil
- 1 tablespoon lemon juice
- 1 tablespoon water
- ¼ teaspoon baking soda
- 1 tablespoon ground cumin
- Salt to taste

Method:

1. Add all the ingredients to a food processor.
2. Process until finely chopped.
3. Form patties from the mixture.
4. Spray your air fryer basket with oil.
5. Add patties to the air fryer basket.
6. Air fry at 375 degrees F for 6 minutes per side.

Serving Suggestions: Serve with toasted bread or cooked brown rice.

Preparation & Cooking Tips: You can use dried chickpeas but soak these overnight first.

Eggplant Parmesan

Preparation Time: 15 minutes
Cooking Time: 17 minutes
Servings: 4

Ingredients:

Breading

- ½ cup breadcrumbs
- ½ teaspoon onion powder
- ½ teaspoon garlic powder
- 1 teaspoon Italian seasoning
- ½ teaspoon dried basil
- ¼ cup Parmesan cheese, grated
- Salt and pepper to taste

Eggplant

- ¼ cup flour
- 2 eggs, beaten
- 1 eggplant, sliced into rounds
- 1 cup reduced-sodium marinara sauce
- 8 slices low-sodium mozzarella cheese

Method:

1. Mix breading ingredients in a bowl.
2. Add flour to another bowl and eggs to a third bowl.
3. Coat eggplant with flour.
4. Dip in egg.
5. Dredge with breading mixture.
6. Preheat your air fryer to 370 degrees F.

7. Add eggplant to the air fryer basket.
8. Cook for 10 minutes.
9. Flip and cook for another 5 minutes.
10. Top with marinara sauce and cheese.
11. Cook for another 2 minutes.

Serving Suggestions: Garnish with chopped parsley.

Preparation & Cooking Tips: Let eggplant rest for 5 minutes before air frying.

Spicy Green Beans

Preparation Time: 20 minutes
Cooking Time: 12 minutes
Servings: 4

Ingredients:

- 12 oz. green beans, trimmed
- 1 clove garlic, minced
- 1 teaspoon soy sauce
- 1 teaspoon rice wine vinegar
- 1 tablespoon sesame oil
- ½ teaspoon crushed red pepper

Method:

1. Preheat your air fryer to 400 degrees F.
2. Add green beans to a bowl.
3. Stir in the remaining ingredients.
4. Marinate for 5 minutes.
5. Air fry for 12 minutes, shaking once or twice.

Serving Suggestions: Serve with garlic mayo dip.

Preparation & Cooking Tips: You can marinate longer for 15 minutes.

Roasted Okra

Preparation Time: 5 minutes
Cooking Time: 12 minutes
Servings: 2

Ingredients:

- 1 lb. okra, trimmed
- 1 teaspoon olive oil
- Garlic powder to taste
- Salt and pepper to taste

Method:

1. Preheat your air fryer to 350 degrees F.
2. Toss okra in oil.
3. Season with garlic powder, salt and pepper.
4. Add to the air fryer.
5. Air fry okra for 5 minutes.
6. Shake and cook for another 5 minutes.
7. Shake once more and cook for 2 minutes.

Serving Suggestions: Drizzle with a little vinegar before serving.

Preparation & Cooking Tips: You can also use garlic salt in place of garlic powder and salt.

Onion Rings

Preparation Time: 15 minutes
Cooking Time: 5 minutes
Servings: 4

Ingredients:

- ¾ cup all-purpose flour
- Salt to taste
- 2 teaspoons baking powder
- ½ cup cornstarch
- 1 large white onion, sliced into rings
- 1 cup milk
- 1 egg, beaten
- 1 cup bread crumbs
- Cooking spray
- Garlic powder to taste

Method:

1. Combine flour, salt, baking powder and cornstarch in a bowl.
2. Coat onion rings with the mixture.
3. Beat egg and milk in another bowl.
4. Dip onion rings in egg mixture.
5. Dredge with breadcrumbs.
6. Preheat your air fryer to 400 degrees F.
7. Add to the air fryer basket.
8. Spray with oil
9. Cook onion rings for 3 to 5 minutes, flipping once.
10. Sprinkle with garlic powder before serving.

Serving Suggestions: Serve with dip of choice.

Preparation & Cooking Tips: You can also season with paprika.

Crispy Green Tomatoes

Preparation Time: 15 minutes
Cooking Time: 15 minutes
Servings: 6

Ingredients:

- 2 green tomatoes, sliced
- Salt and pepper to taste
- ¼ cup all purpose flour
- 2 eggs, beaten
- ½ cup buttermilk
- 1 cup breadcrumbs
- ½ teaspoon paprika
- 1 teaspoon garlic powder
- 1 cup yellow cornmeal
- 1 tablespoon olive oil

Method:

1. Sprinkle tomato with salt and pepper.
2. Add flour to a bowl.
3. Mix eggs and milk to a second bowl.
4. Combine the remaining ingredients except oil to a third bowl.
5. Coat tomatoes with flour.
6. Dip in egg and cover with breadcrumb mixture.
7. Add tomatoes to the air fryer basket.
8. Drizzle with oil.
9. Cook for 12 minutes.
10. Flip and cook for another 3 minutes.

Serving Suggestions: Serve with spicy mayo.

Preparation & Cooking Tips: Cook the tomatoes in batches.

Chapter 8: Snack Recipes

Curried Chickpeas

Preparation Time: 10 minutes
Cooking Time: 15 minutes
Servings: 4

Ingredients:

- 15 oz. unsalted chickpeas, rinsed, drained and skinned
- 2 tablespoons olive oil
- 2 tablespoons red wine vinegar
- Salt to taste
- ¼ teaspoon ground cinnamon
- ½ teaspoon ground turmeric
- 2 teaspoons curry powder
- ¼ teaspoon ground cumin
- ¼ teaspoon ground coriander
- Pinch Aleppo pepper

Method:

1. Toss chickpeas in oil and vinegar.
2. Sprinkle with salt and spices.
3. Add to the air fryer basket.
4. Cook at 400 degrees F for 15 minutes, shaking once halfway through.

Serving Suggestions: Garnish with chopped cilantro.

Preparation & Cooking Tips: You can use red pepper flakes instead of Aleppo pepper.

Pickle Chips

Preparation Time: 10 minutes
Cooking Time: 6 minutes
Servings: 4

Ingredients:

- 16 oz. pickle chips
- ½ cup all purpose flour
- 2 eggs, beaten
- 1 cup breadcrumbs

Dip

- 1 tablespoon mustard
- ¼ cup mayonnaise
- ½ teaspoon smoked paprika
- 1 teaspoon lemon juice

Method:

1. Cover pickle chips with flour.
2. Dip in eggs and dredge with breadcrumbs.
3. Add to the air fryer basket.
4. Air fry at 350 degrees F for 6 minutes.
5. Mix the dip ingredients.
6. Serve pickle chips with dip.

Serving Suggestions: Serve immediately.

Preparation & Cooking Tips: Use Creole mustard if available.

Sesame Kale Chips

Preparation Time: 5 minutes
Cooking Time: 6 minutes
Servings: 2

Ingredients:

- 6 cups kale leaves
- ½ teaspoon garlic, minced
- 1 teaspoon white sesame seeds
- ¼ teaspoon poppy seeds
- 1 teaspoon soy sauce

Method:

1. Combine all the ingredients in a bowl.
2. Add to the air fryer basket.
3. Cook at 375 degrees F for 6 minutes, shaking once.

Serving Suggestions: Serve immediately.

Preparation & Cooking Tips: Dry leaves thoroughly before seasoning.

Potato Chips

Preparation Time: 15 minutes
Cooking Time: 30 minutes
Servings: 4

Ingredients:

- 1 potato, sliced into rounds
- 1 tablespoon oil
- 1 teaspoon rosemary, chopped

Method:

1. Coat potato rounds with oil.
2. Air fry at 375 degrees F for 30 minutes.
3. Sprinkle with rosemary.

Serving Suggestions: Sprinkle with a little salt before serving.

Preparation & Cooking Tips: Potato slices should be 1/8 inch thick.

Roasted Peanuts

Preparation Time: 10 minutes
Cooking Time: 20 minutes
Servings: 8

Ingredients:

- 8 oz. peanuts
- 2 tablespoons olive oil
- ½ teaspoon cayenne pepper
- 3 teaspoons Old Bay seasoning
- Salt to taste

Method:

1. Preheat your air fryer to 320 degrees F.
2. Toss peanuts in olive oil.
3. Season with cayenne pepper, Old Bay seasoning and salt.
4. Place peanuts in the air fryer basket.
5. Cook for 10 minutes.
6. Shake the basket and cook for another 10 minutes.

Serving Suggestions: Drain peanuts after cooking.

Preparation & Cooking Tips: You can also add more cayenne pepper if you like the peanuts spicier.

Fish & Chips

Preparation Time: 20 minutes
Cooking Time: 20 minutes
Servings: 4

Ingredients:

- 2 potatoes, sliced into wedges
- Cooking spray
- Salt to taste
- 1 cup all purpose flour
- 2 eggs, beaten
- 2 tablespoons water
- 1 cup breadcrumbs
- 4 white fish fillets, sliced into strips
- Cooking spray

Method:

1. Add potato wedges to the air fryer basket.
2. Air fry at 375 degrees F for 10 minutes, turning once.
3. Season potato wedges with salt.
4. In a bowl, mix water and eggs.
5. Coat fish fillet strips with flour.
6. Dip in egg mixture, and dredge with breadcrumbs.
7. Spray with oil.
8. Add to the air fryer basket.
9. Cook at 375 degrees F for 10 minutes, flipping once.
10. Serve fish with potato wedges.

Serving Suggestions: Serve with mayo and ketchup.

Preparation & Cooking Tips: Cook in batches.

Greek Feta Fries

Preparation Time: 15 minutes
Cooking Time: 15 minutes
Servings: 2

Ingredients:

- Cooking spray

Fries

- 2 potatoes, sliced into strips
- 1 tablespoon olive oil
- ½ teaspoon dried oregano
- 2 teaspoons lemon zest
- ¼ teaspoon garlic powder
- ¼ teaspoon onion powder
- ¼ teaspoon paprika
- Salt and pepper to taste

Toppings

- 2 oz. chicken breast, cooked and shredded
- 2 oz. feta cheese, grated
- 2 tablespoons red onion, chopped
- ¼ cup tomato, chopped
- 1 tablespoon parsley, chopped
- ¼ cup tzatziki

Method:

1. Preheat your air fryer to 380 degrees F.
2. Spray your air fryer basket with oil.

3. Coat potatoes with olive oil.
4. Season with herbs, spices and salt.
5. Air fry for 15 minutes, flipping once or twice.
6. Transfer to a serving plate.
7. Add remaining ingredients on top.

Serving Suggestions: Serve with sour cream.

Preparation & Cooking Tips: Soak potatoes in cold water for 30 minutes and dry thoroughly before air frying.

Cinnamon Plantain Chips

Preparation Time: 10 minutes
Cooking Time: 10 minutes
Servings: 2

Ingredients:

- 1 plantain, sliced thinly
- Avocado oil spray
- Cinnamon powder to taste

Method:

1. Preheat your air fryer to 350 degrees F.
2. Spray chips with oil.
3. Air fry for 7 minutes.
4. Flip and cook for another 3 minutes.
5. Sprinkle with cinnamon powder.

Serving Suggestions: Sprinkle with a little salt before serving.

Preparation & Cooking Tips: Use green plantain for best results.

Zucchini Chips

Preparation Time: 15 minutes
Cooking Time: 10 minutes
Servings: 8

Ingredients:

- 2 zucchinis, sliced into rounds
- ½ cup cornstarch
- 4 egg whites
- 2 cups breadcrumbs
- Cooking spray
- Salt to taste

Dip

- ½ cup mayonnaise
- 1 cup sour cream
- 2 teaspoons fresh dill, chopped
- 2 tablespoons chives, chopped
- 2 teaspoons lemon juice

Method:

1. Coat zucchini with cornstarch.
2. Dip in egg whites.
3. Dredge with breadcrumbs.
4. Spray zucchini with oil.
5. Air fry at 400 degrees F for 5 minutes.
6. Flip and cook for another 5 minutes.
7. Transfer to a plate.
8. Season with salt.

9. Mix the dip ingredients.
10. Serve with the zucchini chips.

Serving Suggestions: Garnish with fresh dill.

Preparation & Cooking Tips: Use freshly squeezed lemon juice.

Spicy Potato Wedges

Preparation Time: 15 minutes
Cooking Time: 15 minutes
Servings: 4

Ingredients:

- 2 potatoes, sliced into wedges
- 1 ½ tablespoons olive oil
- ½ teaspoon chili powder
- ½ teaspoon parsley flakes
- ½ teaspoon paprika
- Salt and pepper to taste

Method:

1. Preheat your air fryer to 400 degrees F.
2. Toss potatoes in oil.
3. Sprinkle with chili powder, parsley flakes, paprika, salt and pepper.
4. Air fry for 10 minutes.
5. Flip and cook for another 5 minutes.

Serving Suggestions: Serve with ketchup and light mayo.

Preparation & Cooking Tips: Soak potatoes in cold water before air frying but be sure to dry thoroughly with paper towels.

Chapter 9: Appetizer Recipes

Scallops with Bacon

Preparation Time: 15 minutes
Cooking Time: 10 minutes
Servings: 8

Ingredients:

Spicy Mayo

- ½ cup mayonnaise
- 2 tablespoons hot pepper sauce

Scallops

- 1 lb. scallops
- Salt and pepper to taste
- 12 to 15 slices turkey bacon
- Cooking spray

Method:

1. Combine mayo and hot sauce in a bowl. Set aside.
2. Preheat your air fryer to 390 degrees F.
3. Season scallops with salt and pepper.
4. Wrap with turkey bacon.
5. Secure with toothpicks.
6. Spray with oil.
7. Air fry scallops for 7 minutes.
8. Turn and cook for 3 minutes.
9. Serve with spicy mayo.

Serving Suggestions: Garnish with chopped chives.

Preparation & Cooking Tips: Dry scallops thoroughly before seasoning with salt and pepper.

Stuffed Peppers

Preparation Time: 10 minutes
Cooking Time: 10 minutes
Servings: 3

Ingredients:

- 12 oz. ground turkey, cooked
- ¾ cup reduced-sodium marinara sauce
- ¼ cup breadcrumbs
- ½ cup brown rice, cooked
- ¼ cup Parmesan cheese, grated
- Pepper to taste
- 3 tablespoons parsley, chopped
- 3 large red bell peppers, tops sliced off

Method:

1. Mix all the ingredients except bell peppers in a bowl.
2. Stuff mixture into the bell peppers.
3. Cook in the air fryer at 350 degrees F for 10 minutes.

Serving Suggestions: Garnish with chopped chives.

Preparation & Cooking Tips: You can omit rice for low-carb meal.

Tofu Bites

Preparation Time: 15 minutes
Cooking Time: 15 minutes
Servings: 20

Ingredients:

- 8 oz. tofu, sliced into cubes
- 4 tablespoons cornstarch
- 4 tablespoons rice milk (unsweetened)
- ⅛ teaspoon paprika
- ⅛ teaspoon onion powder
- ⅛ teaspoon garlic powder
- Pepper to taste
- ¾ cup breadcrumbs

Method:

1. Coat tofu cubes with cornstarch.
2. Dip in egg.
3. Mix the remaining ingredients.
4. Dredge tofu cubes with breadcrumb mixture.
5. Air fry tofu cubes at 375 degrees F for 15 minutes, flipping twice.

Serving Suggestions: Serve with Buffalo sauce.

Preparation & Cooking Tips: Freeze tofu first and then thaw before slicing and cooking.

Pork Dumplings

Preparation Time: 20 minutes
Cooking Time: 12 minutes
Servings: 6

Ingredients:

Dumplings

- 4 oz. lean ground pork
- 3 cloves garlic, minced
- 1 tablespoon ginger, chopped
- ¼ teaspoon red pepper flakes
- 1 tablespoon scallions, chopped
- 18 wonton wrappers

Sauce

- 2 teaspoons reduced-sodium soy sauce
- 2 tablespoons rice vinegar
- ½ teaspoon brown sugar
- 1 teaspoon sesame oil

Method:

1. Combine dumpling ingredients except wrappers in a bowl.
2. Mix well.
3. Add mixture on top of wrappers.
4. Fold wrappers and seal.
5. Add to the air fryer basket.
6. Air fry at 375 degrees F for 12 minutes.
7. Mix sauce ingredients.
8. Serve dumplings with sauce.

Serving Suggestions: Garnish with chopped chives.

Preparation & Cooking Tips: Cook in batches.

Buffalo Wings

Preparation Time: 20 minutes
Cooking Time: 40 minutes
Servings: 4

Ingredients:

- 4 lb. chicken wings
- ½ teaspoon onion powder
- ½ teaspoon garlic powder
- 1 ½ teaspoons paprika
- Pepper to taste
- 2 tablespoons butter (unsalted)
- ½ cup Buffalo sauce
- ¼ cup ranch dressing

Method:

1. Preheat your oven to 200 degrees F.
2. Preheat your air fryer to 375 degrees F.
3. Season chicken wings with onion powder, garlic powder, paprika and pepper.
4. Marinate for 10 minutes.
5. Add to the air fryer.
6. Air fry for 15 minutes.
7. Flip and cook for another 10 minutes.
8. In a pan over medium heat, mix butter and Buffalo sauce.
9. Simmer for 5 minutes.
10. Toss chicken wings in sauce.
11. Transfer to a baking pan.
12. Bake in the oven for 10 minutes.

Serving Suggestions: Serve with carrot and celery sticks.

Preparation & Cooking Tips: You can also use hot sauce instead of Buffalo sauce.

Egg Rolls

Preparation Time: 20 minutes
Cooking Time: 10 minutes
Servings: 4

Ingredients:

- 5 oz. lean ground pork
- ¼ cup scallions, chopped
- 3 cups cabbage, sliced
- 2 cloves garlic, minced
- 1 teaspoon reduced-sodium soy sauce
- 1 tablespoon lime juice
- 1 egg, beaten
- 6 egg roll wrappers
- Cooking spray

Method:

1. Add all ingredients except wrappers to a bowl.
2. Mix well.
3. Top wrappers with the mixture.
4. Roll up the wrappers and seal.
5. Spray with oil.
6. Air fry at 390 degrees F for 5 minutes per side.

Serving Suggestions: Serve with sweet chili sauce.

Preparation & Cooking Tips: Freeze egg rolls and air fry when ready to serve.

Jalapeño Poppers

Preparation Time: 15 minutes
Cooking Time: 10 minutes
Servings: 4

Ingredients:

- ¼ cup scallion, chopped
- ¼ cup chicken breast, cooked and chopped
- 1 oz. cheddar cheese, shredded
- 2 oz. cream cheese, softened
- 2 teaspoons fresh dill, chopped
- 2 tablespoons hot sauce
- 2 tablespoons breadcrumbs
- 4 jalapeño peppers, sliced in half
- Cooking spray

Method:

1. Mix all the ingredients except jalapeño peppers in a bowl.
2. Top jalapeño peppers with the mixture.
3. Spray with oil.
4. Place in the air fryer basket.
5. Air fry at 370 degrees F for 10 minutes.

Serving Suggestions: Serve with hot sauce.

Preparation & Cooking Tips: You can also use red bell peppers for this recipe.

Sausage Bites

Preparation Time: 15 minutes
Cooking Time: 20 minutes
Servings: 6

Ingredients:

- ⅛ teaspoon ground allspice
- ½ teaspoon ground turmeric
- 3 tablespoons honey
- ½ cup beer
- ½ cup mustard
- 6 sausages, sliced
- 6 sweet peppers, seeded

Method:

1. Add allspice, turmeric, honey and beer to a pan over medium heat.
2. Bring to a boil.
3. Reduce heat and simmer for 10 minutes.
4. Turn off heat and add mustard.
5. Add sausages and sweet peppers in the air fryer basket.
6. Cook at 400 degrees F for 10 minutes.
7. Serve with mustard sauce.

Serving Suggestions: Garnish with chopped chives.

Preparation & Cooking Tips: Use spicy mustard.

Peppers Stuffed with Sausage

Preparation Time: 10 minutes
Cooking Time: 5 minutes
Servings: 20

Ingredients:

- 1 clove garlic, minced
- 8 oz. Italian sausage, removed from casing, cooked and crumbled
- 2 tablespoons blue cheese, crumbled
- ½ cup cheddar cheese, shredded
- 8 oz. cream cheese
- 2 tablespoons breadcrumbs
- Pepper to taste
- 16 oz. large sweet peppers, tops sliced off

Method:

1. Preheat your air fryer to 350 degrees F.
2. Mix garlic, sausage, cheeses, breadcrumbs and peppers in a bowl.
3. Stuff peppers with the mixture.
4. Air fry for 5 minutes.

Serving Suggestions: Garnish with chopped chives.

Preparation & Cooking Tips: You can also use chicken or turkey sausage for this recipe.

Mac & Cheese Balls

Preparation Time: 20 minutes
Cooking Time: 12 minutes
Servings: 4

Ingredients:

- 7 oz. mac and cheese mix (low-sodium), cooked according to package directions
- ¼ cup milk
- 2 tablespoons butter
- ¾ cup cheddar cheese, shredded
- Cooking spray
- Salt to taste
- Pinch garlic powder
- 2 eggs, beaten
- 1 cup breadcrumbs

Method:

1. Preheat your air fryer to 350 degrees F.
2. Mix mac and cheese, milk, butter and cheese in a bowl.
3. Form balls from the mixture.
4. Sprinkle with salt and garlic powder.
5. Dip in eggs and dredge with breadcrumbs.
6. Cook for 8 minutes.
7. Turn and cook for another 4 minutes.

Serving Suggestions: Serve with ketchup.

Preparation & Cooking Tips: Freeze mac and cheese balls and air fry when ready to serve.

Chapter 10: Side Dish Recipes

Roasted Cauliflower & Broccoli

Preparation Time: 15 minutes
Cooking Time: 15 minutes
Servings: 4

Ingredients:

- 2 cups cauliflower florets
- 2 cups broccoli florets
- 1 tablespoon peanut oil
- 3 cloves garlic, minced
- ½ teaspoon paprika
- Salt to taste

Method:

1. Preheat your air fryer to 400 degrees F.
2. Coat the cauliflower and broccoli in oil.
3. Sprinkle with garlic, paprika and salt.
4. Transfer to the air fryer.
5. Cook for 15 minutes, turning every 5 minutes.

Serving Suggestions: Serve with dip of choice.

Preparation & Cooking Tips: You can also use olive oil instead of peanut oil.

Cauliflower Gnocchi

Preparation Time: 10 minutes
Cooking Time: 10 minutes
Servings: 8

Ingredients:

- 20 oz. frozen cauliflower gnocchi
- 3 tablespoons olive oil
- ½ cup Parmesan cheese, grated

Method:

1. Preheat your air fryer to 375 degrees F.
2. Toss gnocchi in the oil and sprinkle with Parmesan cheese.
3. Add to the air fryer basket.
4. Air fry for 5 minutes.
5. Shake and cook for another 5 minutes.

Serving Suggestions: Serve with marinara sauce.

Preparation & Cooking Tips: You can also use this recipe for other types of gnocchi.

Garlic Baby Potatoes

Preparation Time: 10 minutes
Cooking Time: 20 minutes
Servings: 4

Ingredients:

- 1 lb. baby potatoes, sliced in half
- 1 tablespoon avocado oil
- ½ teaspoon granulated garlic
- ½ teaspoon dried parsley flakes
- Salt to taste

Method:

1. Preheat your air fryer to 350 degrees F.
2. Toss the potatoes in oil.
3. Season with garlic, parsley and salt.
4. Cook in the air fryer for 20 minutes, shaking once or twice.

Serving Suggestions: Sprinkle with Parmesan cheese.

Preparation & Cooking Tips: Replace dried parsley with chopped fresh parsley.

Orange & Sesame Tofu

Preparation Time: 10 minutes
Cooking Time: 15 minutes
Servings: 4

Ingredients:

- 28 oz. tofu, sliced into cubes
- Cooking spray
- ¼ cup orange juice
- 2 tablespoons reduced-sodium soy sauce
- 1 tablespoon honey
- 1 teaspoon sesame oil

Method:

1. Air fry tofu cubes at 375 degrees F for 15 minutes, flipping once.
2. In a pan over medium heat, simmer the remaining ingredients for 15 minutes.
3. Toss tofu in the orange sesame sauce before serving.

Serving Suggestions: Garnish with chopped scallions.

Preparation & Cooking Tips: Dry tofu before air frying.

Roasted Butternut Squash

Preparation Time: 10 minutes
Cooking Time: 12 minutes
Servings: 6

Ingredients:

- 2 butternut squash, sliced into cubes
- 2 tablespoons avocado oil
- 2 tablespoons thyme, chopped
- Salt to taste

Method:

1. Toss the squash cubes in oil.
2. Sprinkle with thyme and salt.
3. Add to the air fryer.
4. Cook at 380 degrees F for 12 minutes, turning once.

Serving Suggestions: Drizzle with honey.

Preparation & Cooking Tips: You can also use rosemary instead of thyme.

Conclusion

If you want to have a healthy body, but you don't know how to match the ingredients and what to make food with, Then the Dash Diet Meal Prep for Beginners is perfect for you. Follow this cookbook with straightforward instructions, encouraging advice, and You'll save a lot of time and have a healthy meal plan.

Whether you are Dash dieter or just simply a food lover, This book suits you very well. I'm sure you'll like it. Thank you for buying this book. Now let's start your gourmet journey!

www.ingramcontent.com/pod-product-compliance
Lightning Source LLC
Chambersburg PA
CBHW081403070526
44583CB00020B/2657